D0495353

Geography
Success

3

Terry Jennings

DANUBE INTERNATIONAL
SCHOOL VIENNA
A-1020 Wien, Josef-Gall-Gasse 2
Tel. ...

OXFORD
UNIVERSITY PRESS

Acknowledgements

The author and publisher would like to thank the following for help in the preparation of this book:

Jeremy and Lourdes Cottam; Brenda Miles.

Photographic credits

Alamy/WGPR p 30 (bottom); Courtesy of Dover Harbour Board p 48; Corbis/Neil Rabinowitz p 37; Ecoscene/Rod Smith p 28 (top); English Heritage p 49; Eye Ubiquitous/A J G Bell p 43 (right) /Nick Bonetti p 13 /David Cumming pp 19, 51 /Laurence Fordyce p 6 (bottom) /Steve Lindridge p 50 /Tim Page p 18 (top) /David Peez p 18 (bottom) /Bryan Pickering p 36 /J B Pickering p 25 /Stephen Rafferty p 54 /Paul Thompson p 43 (left) /Gary Trotter p 31; Getty Images/Richard Elliott p 40; Greg Evans International p 32; Courtesy of Hutchison Ports (UK) Limited p 47 (right); ICCE/Tom Skitt p 21 /Philip Steele p 20 (bottom); James Davis Worldwide pp 12 (bottom), 44; Terry Jennings pp 7, 8, 10, 12 (top), 16 (both), 33, 38 (all), 39, 47 (left), 52, 53, 55 (both); PA Photos/EPA pp 17, 57, 58 (both) /Tim Ockenden p 30 (top) /Kirsty Wigglesworth p 22 (right); Science Photo Library/J G Golden p 59; Skyscan/Bob Evans p 45 /NOAA p 56; Stills Pictures p 15; www.tografox.com/R D Battersby pp 4 (both), 22 (left), 24, 27, 28 (bottom), 29, 32 (top), 40 (top), 41; Travel Ink p 20 (top).

Cover photo: Pablo Corral V/Corbis

Maps (pp 6, 42, 44, 46, 48, 50, 60, 61) © GEOATLAS 1998, 1999 Graphi-Ogre

OXFORD
UNIVERSITY PRESS

Great Clarendon Street, Oxford OX2 6DP

Oxford University Press is a department of the University of Oxford. It furthers the University's objective of excellence in research, scholarship, and education by publishing worldwide in

Oxford New York

Auckland Cape Town Dar es Salaam Hong Kong Karachi Kuala Lumpur Madrid Melbourne Mexico City Nairobi New Delhi Shanghai Taipei Toronto

With offices in

Argentina Austria Brazil Chile Czech Republic France Greece Guatemala Hungary Italy Japan Poland Portugal Singapore South Korea Switzerland Thailand Turkey Ukraine

Oxford is a registered trade mark of Oxford University Press in the UK and certain other countries

© Terry Jennings 2002

The moral rights of the author have been asserted

Database right Oxford University Press (maker)

First published 2002

All rights reserved. No part of this publication may be reproduced, stored in a retrieval system, or transmitted, in any form or by any means, without the prior permission in writing of Oxford University Press, or as expressly permitted by law, or under terms agreed with the appropriate reprographics rights organization. Enquiries concerning reproduction outside the scope of the above should be sent to the Rights Department, Oxford University Press, at the address above.

You must not circulate this book in any other binding or cover and you must impose this same condition on any acquirer

British Library Cataloguing in Publication Data

Data available

ISBN 13 9780198338451

ISBN 0 19 833845 7

10 9 8

Editorial, design and picture research by Lodestone Publishing Limited, Uckfield, East Sussex www.lodestonepublishing.com

Illustrations by James Browne, Chapman Bounford and Associates, Michael Eaton, Miller, Craig & Cocking, The Tudor Art Agency (London) Limited

Language and teaching consultant: Anne Mepham

Printed by Gráficas Estella, Spain

Contents

(and suggested order of teaching)

YEAR 5

We need water

What would life be like without water? Water is one of the most important substances on Earth. Without water to drink we would die. About 70 per cent of our body weight is water. People have lived for a month or more without food, but no one can live for more than three or four days without water.

How do we use water? We wash many things with water. We use water to flush the toilet. The foods we eat have water in them and all our drinks are largely water. We also use water to cook many of our foods.

We need water to keep ourselves clean.

Animals, plants and water

Animals and plants need water to live. Some simple plants and animals are 99 per cent water. Plants take up water from the soil through their roots. The animals that provide us with meat, milk and eggs need large amounts of clean water to drink. Water is also home to millions of plants and animals, including one of our most important foods – fish.

Crops and irrigation

Farmers all around the world need water for their crops.

How much water do animals and plants need?	
human	2 litres per day
dairy cow	135 litres per day
oak tree	20 000 litres per day

In some places, where there is not much rain and the land is dry, farmers bring water to their fields. The water is carried to the fields in pipes and ditches from rivers, **lakes** and **wells**. This special kind of watering is called **irrigation**. Some crops need more water to grow than others. Rice and cotton, for example, can be grown only in countries that are very hot and which also have lots of rain.

How does industry use water?

In some **industries**, water is used to cool the moving parts of machinery or hot substances.

Water is used to help produce most of our electricity. All **power stations** that burn fuels use water to make steam to turn the machines that produce electricity. In hydro-electric power stations, the water of fast-flowing rivers is used to turn the machines that produce electricity.

Water is used to make many of the things we see or use every day. Making cement, concrete, steel and paper uses huge quantities of water. Water is also used to make many kinds of food.

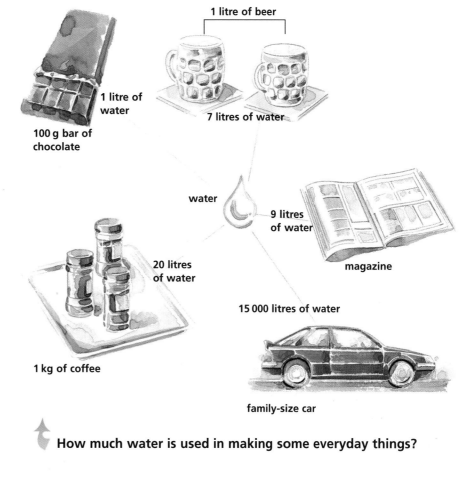

1 litre of beer

1 litre of water

100 g bar of chocolate

7 litres of water

water

9 litres of water

magazine

20 litres of water

15 000 litres of water

1 kg of coffee

family-size car

How much water is used in making some everyday things?

Activities

1 Keep a diary of all the ways you use water during a whole week. Examples include washing your hands, flushing the toilet and watering plants.
   a Record your results on a spreadsheet.
   b Discuss your results with your class. How could you use less water?

2 Imagine you are going to a faraway planet. There is no water on the planet, so you will have to take supplies with you. Draw or write about what you will need water for.

3 How is water used for people to enjoy themselves in your area? Make a list of the places where water is used for leisure activities. Draw pictures to show the different places.

Water everywhere

Look at a globe or the map of the world on page 61. How much of the Earth do you think is covered by water?

Nearly three-quarters of the Earth is covered by water, but most of it is salty seawater.

Oceans

There is water in the **oceans**. What are the five great oceans? The largest ocean in the world is the Pacific Ocean. It covers about a third of the surface of the Earth and its average depth is over 4000 m. All the oceans are connected to each other. This means that their waters are mixed together.

Seas

In addition to the oceans, there are **seas**. Some of these, such as the Arabian Sea and the Sargasso Sea, are parts of oceans. The largest of the world's seas is the South China Sea. Other seas are surrounded by land on the **continents**, and so are separate from the oceans. The Red Sea, Mediterranean Sea and Black Sea are all on continents, although the Mediterranean does have a narrow opening into the Atlantic Ocean. How many seas can you find on a world map?

The water in the oceans and seas is always salty. Some of this salt has come from volcanoes under the sea, but most of it has **dissolved** from rocks on land.

Fresh water

Where else, besides oceans and seas, is there water in the world? Most of the water we need for drinking, washing, cooking and growing plants comes from lakes and rivers. This is called fresh water. It is not salty like seawater.

Some fresh water is found in the form of ice. Ice can be found on the tops of high mountains. Sometimes the ice flows down the mountainside, like a slow-moving river. Such rivers of ice are called **glaciers**.

There are huge sheets of ice, called polar ice caps, around the North and South Poles. The picture shows the Antarctic polar ice cap.

Did you know that there are huge quantities of fresh water under the ground? Every time it rains, some of the rainwater soaks into the ground and through tiny cracks in rocks. Sometimes the water flows as an underground river.

There is also a small proportion of the world's water in the air. Some of it we can see, as clouds, but much of it is the invisible gas called **water vapour**.

Do you think this lake in Austria is fresh water or salt water?

Although there are huge quantities of water in the world, about 97 per cent of it is salty. Only about 3 per cent of the world's water is fresh, coming from lakes, rivers, streams, ice, clouds or water vapour.

Activities

1 Here is a map quiz. Use an atlas to help you to answer the questions.
   a What is the name of the ocean off the west coasts of the British Isles, France and Portugal?
   b What is the name of the sea between Britain and Ireland?
   c What is the name of the sea between Japan and North Korea?
   d What is the name of the ocean to the east of Africa?
   e Find three seas which have colours in their name.

f Which oceans and seas would a ship cross if it sailed from Sydney, Australia, to London, England, by the shortest route?

2 Make a sketch plan of your school and its grounds. Walk around the school and mark on your plan all the places where water moves, including any taps, gutters and downpipes.

3 Use an atlas to find five countries with a very high rainfall and five countries with a very low rainfall. Compare your results with those of your classmates.

The water supply

What do we need clean water for? In one year the average family of four uses about 210 000 litres of water – enough to fill four large tanker lorries to overflowing. If we are to stay healthy, this water has to be clean and safe to use.

Where does our water come from?

All the water we use comes from rain (or snow in winter). Many people in the world still have to collect their water from a stream or well. However, in places where there are lots of people, such as in towns and cities, local streams and wells cannot provide enough water for the population. Water has to be **transported** from lakes, rivers or **reservoirs** further away.

A reservoir is a large, artificial lake made by building a **dam** across a river. Wherever possible, reservoirs are built high up in hills or mountains where they are filled by water from clean rivers and streams. This reservoir is in the Welsh mountains.

Water treatment

Do you know how water is cleaned? Where is it cleaned in your area?

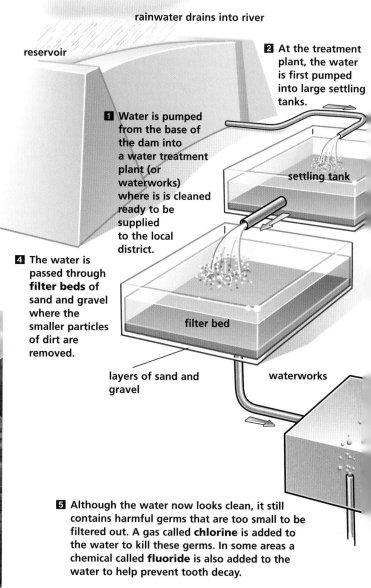

rainwater drains into river

reservoir

1 Water is pumped from the base of the dam into a water treatment plant (or waterworks) where is is cleaned ready to be supplied to the local district.

2 At the treatment plant, the water is first pumped into large settling tanks.

settling tank

4 The water is passed through **filter beds** of sand and gravel where the smaller particles of dirt are removed.

filter bed

layers of sand and gravel

waterworks

5 Although the water now looks clean, it still contains harmful germs that are too small to be filtered out. A gas called **chlorine** is added to the water to kill these germs. In some areas a chemical called **fluoride** is also added to the water to help prevent tooth decay.

Sewage

Used water from homes, schools and factories is normally passed through big pipes called sewers, to a **sewage** works for cleaning. The cleaned-up water may then be returned to a river or pumped into the sea.

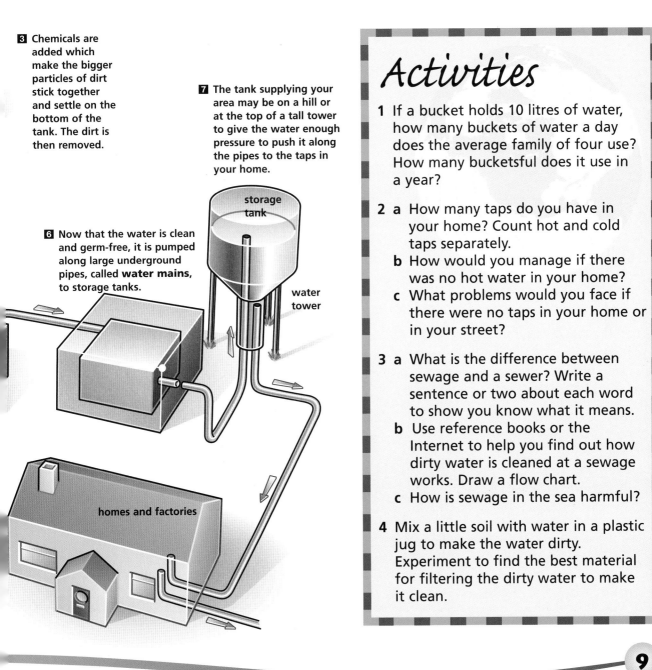

3 Chemicals are added which make the bigger particles of dirt stick together and settle on the bottom of the tank. The dirt is then removed.

7 The tank supplying your area may be on a hill or at the top of a tall tower to give the water enough pressure to push it along the pipes to the taps in your home.

6 Now that the water is clean and germ-free, it is pumped along large underground pipes, called **water mains**, to storage tanks.

storage tank

water tower

homes and factories

Activities

1 If a bucket holds 10 litres of water, how many buckets of water a day does the average family of four use? How many bucketsful does it use in a year?

2 a How many taps do you have in your home? Count hot and cold taps separately.
  b How would you manage if there was no hot water in your home?
  c What problems would you face if there were no taps in your home or in your street?

3 a What is the difference between sewage and a sewer? Write a sentence or two about each word to show you know what it means.
  b Use reference books or the Internet to help you find out how dirty water is cleaned at a sewage works. Draw a flow chart.
  c How is sewage in the sea harmful?

4 Mix a little soil with water in a plastic jug to make the water dirty. Experiment to find the best material for filtering the dirty water to make it clean.

Deserts

What is a desert? The driest places in the world are deserts. Deserts are dry lands where very little rain falls and where few plants can grow. Scientists usually say that an area is a desert if an average of less that 250 mm of rain falls each year. More than one-seventh of the land on Earth is taken up by desert.

Kinds of desert

There are two kinds of desert:

- Very cold deserts: found in the Arctic and Antarctic regions at the North and South Poles. The ground is covered with ice and snow for all or most of the year.

- Hot deserts: mostly sunny and very dry although they can be very cold at night.

The map shows where the great hot deserts of the world are found.

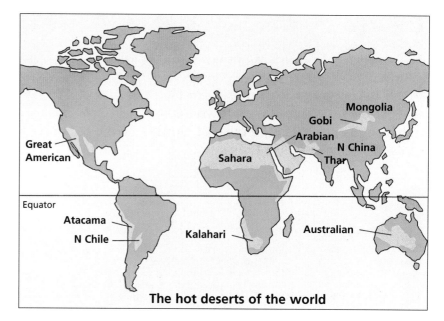

The hot deserts of the world

Desert scenery

Many people think of hot deserts as being sandy, with the **sand** blown into hilly **dunes** by the wind. But in most hot deserts, the wind has blown the sand away, leaving pebbles or even bare rock. Shallow lakes form in some deserts after rain. When the water **evaporates**, only a flat layer of salt is left. Elsewhere there are mountains and steep rocky slopes. Some of these have been carved into interesting shapes by the wind.

These dunes are in the world's largest hot desert – the Sahara Desert in North Africa.

Desert plants

The few plants that are able to survive in the desert have to **adapt** to the dry conditions. Some desert plants have long roots to reach water deep underground. The roots of the acacia tree of Africa may go down 30 m or more to reach water, while the mesquite bush of North America sends its roots down to a depth of 50 m.

Desert animals

Few animals live in the desert. Those that can survive get the water they need from their food. Most of them sleep during the day and come out only at night when it is cooler.

The best-known desert animal is the camel. A camel can go a long time without drinking water. It can lose about one-third of the weight of its body and still live. Then, when the camel does find water, it can drink 115 litres or more in a few minutes.

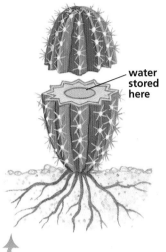

water stored here

A cactus plant stores water in its thick stem. As the cactus gradually uses up the water, the stem shrivels. When the next rain comes, the cactus stores more water.

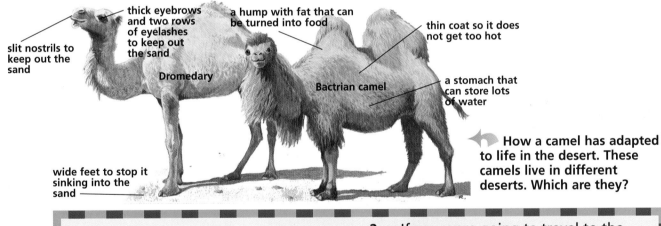

thick eyebrows and two rows of eyelashes to keep out the sand

a hump with fat that can be turned into food

thin coat so it does not get too hot

slit nostrils to keep out the sand

Dromedary

Bactrian camel

a stomach that can store lots of water

wide feet to stop it sinking into the sand

How a camel has adapted to life in the desert. These camels live in different deserts. Which are they?

Activities

1 In the Sahara Desert in summer, temperatures of 58 °C in the shade have been recorded.
Measure the differences between the temperatures in the sunshine and in the shade on a hot day.
Record your results.

2 a If you were going to travel to the Sahara Desert, list the things you would take with you. Arrange your list in order of importance.
  b What problems would you meet in the desert? How would you cope with them?

3 Make and illustrate a book or class display on plant and animal life in deserts. Use reference books or the Internet to help you.

Desert peoples

In most parts of the world there is a lot of water under the ground. This is known as **groundwater**. Each time it rains, some of the water seeps down into the ground where it fills all the cracks and openings in the rocks below. Often, it is possible to dig a well to reach this water.

Desert oases

In deserts, most of the water from rain is lost. It either runs off the hard, dry surface or evaporates into the air. A little of it soaks into the ground where it may eventually join underground rivers and streams. Some of these rivers and streams bring water from mountains hundreds of kilometres away, where there is heavy rainfall or snow.

In a few places, water from these underground rivers or streams flows to the surface of the desert. The water forms a **spring** or **waterhole**, making the land **fertile** so plants can grow. This is called an **oasis**. A river flowing through a desert may have long oases along its banks.

In this oasis in the Sahara Desert, people are able to grow crops by irrigating them with water pumped from a well.

These nomadic Bedouins are in the Syrian Desert. The Bedouin have no fixed homes. Instead, they live in tents made from goat or camel skins. To protect themselves from the heat, cold and wind-blown sand, they wear long, flowing robes.

Oasis peoples

Towns and villages are built around oases and waterholes in the desert. The people who live in an oasis village make use of every bit of fertile land. In the oases of the Sahara Desert, for example, the people grow food plants such as vegetables, dates, figs, olives and apricots. They keep cattle, sheep and goats for their meat and milk.

Nomadic peoples

People who live in oases are not the only people who live in the desert. Wanderers, or **nomads**, also live there. Some of the Bedouin of the Sahara and Arabian Deserts are nomads. They travel from one oasis to another, driving their herds of sheep and goats in front of them. The sheep and goats feed on the scattered desert plants. Because it is so hot during the day, the Bedouin often travel at night when it is cool, and rest during the daytime.

Much of the time, the Bedouin live mainly on camel's milk, cheese and dates. They visit oases to exchange meat, skins and handicrafts for tea, dates, rice and other foods. They also let their camels drink water there.

Some of the Mongol people of the Gobi desert in Asia are also nomads. The nomadic Mongols are herdsmen, keeping horses, sheep, cattle, goats and camels. They ride short-legged, long-haired horses when they round up or drive their herds of animals.

Today, many of the Bedouin and Mongol peoples have been encouraged to change to a more settled existence. This is partly because governments find it difficult to control people when they travel around, crossing from one country to another.

This Mongol encampment is in the Gobi Desert in Asia. The round tents are called *gers*. They are made from thick **felt** stretched over a wooden frame.

Activities

1 Nomads do not build permanent homes. Why do you think this is?

2 a What kinds of clothes do people wear in the desert?
   b What colours are they?
   c What materials are the clothes made from?
   Draw pictures of the different kinds of clothes people wear.

3 Use reference books or the Internet to find out about the kinds of homes people have in desert areas.
   a What are the homes made of?
   b Why are so many houses in desert areas painted white?
   c Why do they often have thick walls and small windows?

4 Collect pictures of the different kinds of desert house and make a class display of them.

Tropical rainforests

Some of the wettest places on Earth are **tropical rainforests**. In the rainforests it is hot and there is a great deal of rain all the year round. The rainfall often averages more than 2500 mm a year.

Many useful things, like rubber, Brazil nuts, bananas, nutmeg and some medicines, come from tropical rainforests. So do some of our most valuable **hardwoods**, including teak, mahogany and rosewood.

Where are the rainforests?

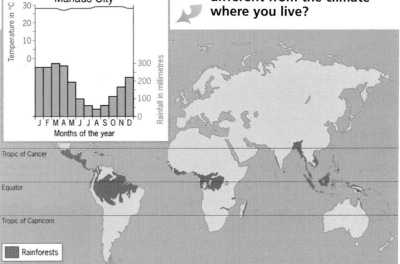

The graph shows temperature and rainfall for a city in the Amazon rainforest. How is the **climate** of the rainforest different from the climate where you live?

This map shows where the world's tropical rainforests are found. Where is the largest area of rainforest?

Rainforest trees

The trees in a rainforest are very large and close together. The trees are evergreen and, as they grow all the year round, there are always flowers, fruits, leaves and nuts for animals to eat. As a result, there are more kinds of wildlife in a rainforest than in any other kind of **environment**. Although tropical rainforests take up only about 7 per cent of the world's land area, they are home to almost half of the different kinds of plants and animals in the world.

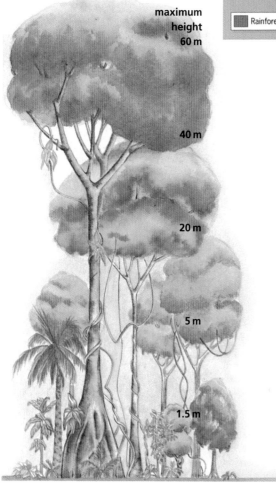

A tropical rainforest is built up of different layers of trees, shrubs and other plants.

Rainforest peoples

Tropical rainforests are home to many small tribes of native people who are experts at living in the rainforest and obtaining everything they need from it. These are Yanomami farming people who live in the rainforest of Brazil in South America. The native people have little long-term effect on their environment.

Threatened rainforests

Unfortunately, the world's tropical rainforests are under threat. Huge areas are being cleared to obtain valuable timber or to make way for:

- mines
- factories
- roads
- large farms (called ranches)
- **plantations**.

The people and wildlife that live in the rainforest will lose their homes. Some scientists believe that the destruction of the tropical rainforests is also affecting the world's **climate**.

Activities

1 Work with a friend. Discuss why so few people live in the tropical rainforests. Write down your conclusions.

2 Make a chart to compare your local area with a tropical rainforest area. Use these headings: Weather, Plants, Animals, Landscape, People.

3 Study an individual continent where tropical rainforests are found, such as Africa or South America.
   a What different types of climate are found there?
   b How does the climate affect the type of clothes people wear, the way they build their houses, the different crops they grow and the domestic animals they rear?

Drought

Some countries have too much rain and there are regular floods. What happens when there is too little rain?

A **drought** is a long period of dry **weather**, when no rain falls for weeks, months or even years. In the deserts there is drought all the time.

Regular droughts

Many parts of the world have a period of drought every year. These are the places which have a dry season and a wet season. The countries around the Mediterranean Sea, for example, have rains in winter and droughts in summer. People plan for the dry period by storing water and by growing crops that can survive in the dry weather.

Unexpected droughts

The worst droughts are those that are not expected. In tropical areas, if the rains fail to arrive, there is no water to store for the dry season.

Crops, such as these sugar beet plants, wither and die during a drought.

Drought causes rivers, lakes, reservoirs and wells to dry up. Plants wither and die. Animals trample the ground down hard as they search for plants to eat and water to drink. The animals die, or their owners kill and eat them. The soil becomes as dry as dust and is blown away in strong winds. In the hot sunshine, the dry plants and bushes may catch fire. Even when the rains return, crops will not grow well.

With no crops for food, and no animals left to provide meat or milk, country people starve unless they can get food from somewhere else. People who live in towns and cities are affected, too, because, when food is in short supply, prices rise and it becomes too expensive for some people to buy.

During a long drought, animals die of starvation and lack of water. This giraffe died during a drought in Kenya.

Drought and famine

What happens when there is a long drought? In the poorer countries of the world, a long drought often leads to **famine**. A famine is when a large number of people do not have enough to eat. During a famine, people become weaker and weaker, and are unable to fight off disease. Children and mothers starve, and babies die as their mother's milk dries up.

The region around the southern edge of the Sahara Desert suffered a severe drought in the 1980s. This led to a terrible famine in which about 2 million people died of starvation.

Another severe drought struck the Orissa region in India, in 1998. There had been very little rain for several years, and then, in 1998, the **monsoon** rains failed to arrive. Crops withered and died and more than half a million people had to leave their homes in search of food elsewhere. Many starved to death.

These people are waiting for food and medicines at a famine relief camp in Sudan.

Activities

1 Mark on a large map of the world areas where drought and famine are in the news. Make a key to your map.

2 Imagine there is a drought where you live. How many ways of saving water can you think of? Write them down in order of importance.

3 Some newspapers show the daily amount of rainfall for large towns and cities.
 a Collect these figures for a week and record them on a chart.
 b Make a league table with the wettest town or city at the top and the driest at the bottom.
 c Use an atlas to help you mark these towns and cities on a map. What do you notice?

Safe water

Where does our water come from? We tend to take water for granted. We can turn on a tap and have water to drink or wash with. When we flush the toilet, water washes away our waste. But at least two-thirds of the people in the world do not have a tap inside their home. They have to obtain water from a tap, well, waterhole, stream or river some distance away. Their toilet may be a bucket, a hole in the ground, or a river.

How much water do we use?

How much water we use depends on how easy it is to obtain. In the poorer countries of the world, many people have to make do with only a few litres of water a day. This water may have come from a river or waterhole which has been used as a toilet by people and animals.

Collecting water from a well in Sri Lanka

Water used per person per day	
Africa	30 litres
Europe	200 litres
United States	600 litres

Fetching water

How do we get our water? In the poorer parts of some countries, it is the work of women and children to fetch water for the family to use. For most women, carrying water takes up several hours of every day. In the very dry areas south of the Sahara Desert, on average, women spend two to three hours each day walking to a waterhole 12 km from their home, and back again. On the return journey, each woman carries the water on her head in a clay pot which weighs about 25 kg when full. In parts of East Africa, children have to get up at three o'clock in the morning and walk 12 km to fetch water.

In country areas of India, a woman may work for 20 hours each day, spending, on average, about five hours of this fetching and carrying water.

Water and disease

What makes water dirty?

In Britain, the water that comes from the taps is clean and free from germs. But for people in many countries, the water they drink, cook or wash themselves with, can make them ill and cause diseases such as cholera, typhoid, dysentery and diarrhoea. Scientists believe that eight out of ten sick people in poorer countries have diseases that have been spread by water. Every day, about 70 000 children die from diseases spread by drinking or using water that has been **polluted** by sewage.

Men washing clothes, dishes and themselves in the polluted waters of the Hooghly River in Kolkata, India

Activities

1 Work in a group of friends. Pour 5 litres of water into a bucket. Take turns to carry it around the playground.
   a Ask each of your friends how much they think the bucket of water weighs. Record their answers.
   b Now weigh the bucket of water. Whose guess was nearest?
   c Imagine you had to carry the bucket of water 12 km. Write down how you think you would feel.

2 Imagine you had to collect all the water for your family from a well at the other end of your street. How would this change life in your home?

3 Find out more about cholera from reference books or the Internet. Find the names of two countries where people still suffer from cholera.

Who owns water?

Although the water you use originally fell from the sky as rain, you have to pay for it, unless you get your water from a well in your own garden. Nearly every home in Britain receives a bill from the local water company demanding payment for the water supplied to it. Many homes have a meter that measures how much water has been used.

Special bamboo pipes are used to collect rainwater in this village in Laos.

The cost

Why do we have to pay for water? It costs a lot of money to build dams and reservoirs, waterworks, water towers and all the **water mains** and pipes that carry water to our homes. The cost of cleaning and **purifying** the water that comes from our taps also has to be paid for. And when we have used the water, we have to pay towards the cost of the pipes and sewage works that clean the water and make it fit to put back into a river or the sea.

In a few places, solar panels, which produce electricity from sunlight, are used to drive pumps that bring up water from deep underground. This solar-powered water pump is in The Gambia, Africa.

Unsafe water

In the poorer countries of the world, many people do not have enough money to pay for clean water. Some people have to take their water from polluted wells, streams and waterholes. In these places, too, few homes or villages have a safe toilet. Frequently, people have to use an open pit or a bucket that may overflow into the local well, river or stream.

Charities and water

Many charities are working in poorer countries to try to provide clean water and safe toilets. Charities, such as Save the Children, Oxfam, Christian Aid and Water Aid, are drilling wells deep into the ground, in places where the underground water is clean and safe to use. Unlike the wells built by local people, which are often shallow and dug by hand, these new wells are lined with piping and covered so that the water does not become polluted.

In countries that are not too dry, small dams and reservoirs are being built.

Charities are building **latrines** in country areas. A latrine is a kind of toilet used where there are no sewers or running water. The pit latrine has a special pipe which removes flies and bad smells so that it is not too unpleasant to use. This latrine is in Zimbabwe, Africa.

Activities

1 Design a poster to help to raise money for a water project in a country where there is a shortage of clean, safe water.

2 Look at a water bill for your home. How is the amount you have to pay worked out? What kinds of things does the water company charge for?

3 You can work out how much water a dripping tap wastes. Turn on the cold tap until it is just dripping. Put a bucket under the tap and measure how much water drips into the bucket in an hour. How much water would drip away in **a** a day, **b** a week, **c** a year?

4 Work with a friend. Discuss how other countries can help those that regularly have water shortages. Write down your ideas.

5 Find out more about some of the charities that are working to improve the supplies of fresh, clean water to some of the world's poorer countries. Use as many sources of information as you can.

Transport

In the past, most people walked or travelled by horse or some other animal when they made a journey. In some parts of the world, these are still the only methods of travel for many people.

Different forms of transport

Which forms of **transport** have you used? In Britain today, the most common forms of transport are bicycles, cars, buses, vans, lorries, trains, aeroplanes and ships. These are all ways of taking people or goods from one place to another.

Day and night, all over the world, millions of people and huge quantities of goods are moving from one place to another. The different forms of transport follow fixed routes. Motor **vehicles** travel along roads and **motorways**, trains run on railway lines, aircraft follow **flight paths** and ships keep to special shipping **lanes**.

Why is transport important?

A good transport system is important to us. We expect to have our letters delivered, and food and other goods delivered to the shops. Factories need a steady supply of **raw materials** and some means of carrying away the goods they have produced. Many people travel to other countries for their work or for their holidays. There is now hardly anywhere in the world we cannot reach in 24 hours. And wherever we are, in an emergency we expect the fire brigade, ambulance or police to come to our aid quickly.

What are the advantages and disadvantages of each form of transport?

Bicycles are inexpensive and quiet and do not pollute the air.

They are not good for long journeys, and not very comfortable in bad weather.

Motor vehicles can go to many different places and move people and goods easily.

However, they are noisy, they pollute the air and can be dangerous, particularly to **pedestrians** and cyclists.

Trains link big towns and cities and can carry lots of people or heavy goods.

They are noisy if you happen to live near a railway, and there are many places they cannot reach because there are no railway lines.

It is often necessary to use some other form of transport to get to and from a railway station.

Land and buildings

All forms of transport require special **routeways** and, sometimes, buildings too. Bicycles and motor vehicles need roads or motorways, while trains need railway lines and railway stations. Ships need special harbours and docks, and aeroplanes need airports with road and rail links to them.

Activities

1 London's Heathrow Airport is the busiest airport in the British Isles.
   a Use maps and local information or the Internet to find out where the major routeways into and out of the airport go. Do they pass through towns and villages, or do they go around them?
   b Now do the same for the major airport nearest to your area.

2 On a map of your local area, mark the following public services:
   fire station   police station
   hospital   health centre
   clinic or doctors' surgery

a On your map, work out a route a fire engine would take from the fire station to your school. Label any important information such as 'one way street' or 'traffic lights'. Remember that the shortest route might not be the quickest for a large fire engine.
b Now repeat this for the other services.

3 Work with a friend and an atlas. Discuss which kind of transport would be best for bringing the following to your area:
   a people from Paris
   b crude oil from Saudi Arabia
   c letters from New Zealand
   d oranges from southern Spain
   e new motor cars from Japan.

Ships and boats can cross oceans and seas carrying large numbers of passengers and huge quantities of cargo.

They are slow and can travel only from one port to another, on a river, lake or sea coast.

Aeroplanes are the fastest way of travelling. They can cross mountains, oceans and seas, as well as land.

They can carry large numbers of people, but not very large or heavy cargoes.

They are also noisy and pollute the air.

There are not very many airports, so people may have to travel a long way by road or rail to get to an airport.

Road traffic

The first roads were bumpy, twisting, narrow, muddy tracks used by people and their herds of animals. About 2000 years ago, the Romans built straight roads in Europe and North Africa so that soldiers could march easily from one part of the Roman Empire to another. Roman roads were paved with stones, and had a sloping surface to allow rainwater to drain away.

What are roads like today?

Today, in Britain, many country roads follow the routes of the first tracks. They twist and turn around people's property and other obstacles such as ponds and woods.

The most important roads in Britain today are called motorways. On a long journey in Britain, most people will travel along a motorway at some time. A motorway is named with the letter M, followed by a number, such as M1, M9 and M27. Motorways have two or more lanes in each direction, separated by a central barrier. They have no sharp bends, steep hills, crossroads, roundabouts or traffic lights.

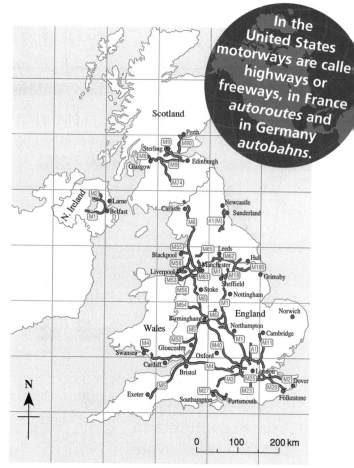

In the United States motorways are called highways or freeways, in France autoroutes and in Germany autobahns.

Cars, lorries, vans and coaches can usually travel quickly along a motorway.

'A' roads and minor roads

Other important main roads are called 'A' roads, such as A1, A5, A30 and A947. Many 'A' roads have just one lane in each direction. Some have two or more lanes in each direction, when they are called **dual carriageways**. Many modern dual-carriageway 'A' roads are built like motorways, but others have traffic lights, crossroads, roundabouts and steep hills.

Roads that are not as important as motorways and 'A' roads are called minor roads. Some of the larger minor roads have names like B1113 or B723, but many do not have names.

Traffic on the A61 in Sheffield

Roads and development

Good roads are important to an area. Factories and shops need a good road **network** to move their goods. If an area has good roads, new factories, offices and shops may be built there, attracting new jobs.

Most factories and many supermarkets and other large stores are now built on the outskirts of a town or city, where roads are less busy than those nearer the middle.

Houses, schools and hospitals need a good road network. Why do you think this is important?

Activities

1 Look at a map of your local area.
 a What types of road are there? Now look at a road atlas and follow the routes that these roads take.
 b Which towns and cities do they pass through?
 c How long is each road?
 d Record your results on a spreadsheet.

2 Draw a sketch map of the area where you live. Show all the motorways, A roads and B roads. Label the roads with their correct names. Make a key for your map.

3 All roads have speed limits. Use the Highway Code, or reference books or the Internet, to find out what are the maximum speed limits on the different types of road.

4 Make a table showing the advantages and disadvantages of cars as a method of transport.

25

Traffic problems

What is the main method of transport today? In developed countries, people use cars more than any other kind of transport. Lorries and vans are the main methods of moving goods from place to place.

In London in 2000, the average speed of traffic was 20 km per hour – the same as it was in 1900 when horses were the main method of transport.

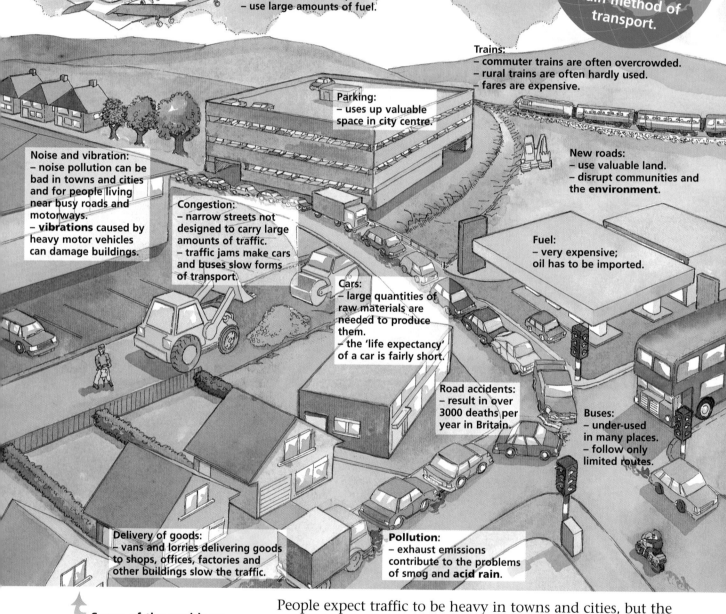

Aeroplanes:
– cause noise and air pollution.
– use large amounts of fuel.

Trains:
– commuter trains are often overcrowded.
– rural trains are often hardly used.
– fares are expensive.

Parking:
– uses up valuable space in city centre.

Noise and vibration:
– noise pollution can be bad in towns and cities and for people living near busy roads and motorways.
– **vibrations** caused by heavy motor vehicles can damage buildings.

New roads:
– use valuable land.
– disrupt communities and the **environment**.

Congestion:
– narrow streets not designed to carry large amounts of traffic.
– traffic jams make cars and buses slow forms of transport.

Fuel:
– very expensive; oil has to be imported.

Cars:
– large quantities of raw materials are needed to produce them.
– the 'life expectancy' of a car is fairly short.

Road accidents:
– result in over 3000 deaths per year in Britain.

Buses:
– under-used in many places.
– follow only limited routes.

Delivery of goods:
– vans and lorries delivering goods to shops, offices, factories and other buildings slow the traffic.

Pollution:
– exhaust emissions contribute to the problems of smog and **acid rain**.

Some of the problems caused by traffic

People expect traffic to be heavy in towns and cities, but the situation is not much better in country areas. Winding, narrow country roads were not built for today's large lorries or fast cars. Many villages also suffer from drivers using their roads as a short-cut to the nearest motorway or 'A' road.

Why is this police officer wearing a mask?

Air pollution

Motor vehicles also pollute the air with fumes from their exhaust pipes. These fumes contain:

- soot which dirties buildings and damages the lungs of people who breathe it in

- carbon monoxide – a gas that prevents oxygen being taken into the body, and helps to cause an unhealthy mixture of smoke and fog, called smog

- nitrogen oxides – gases that help to cause acid rain and also **global warming** (or the greenhouse effect) by trapping the Sun's heat; they also cause breathing problems in humans

- hydrocarbons – gases that may cause cancer and breathing problems, and also help to cause global warming.

One child in seven in Britain now suffers from asthma or other breathing difficulties, which many people believe are caused, or made worse, by air pollution. In addition to the noise and air pollution caused by motor vehicles, many people are killed or injured in road accidents.

Activities

1 Ask your teacher to organize a class visit to a local high street area. Look at and record information about any traffic problems and how they affect people and businesses. Record your results on graphs.

2 Work with a group of friends. Discuss the ways in which planners try to solve traffic problems. Which of these ways are the most effective? Which are least effective?

3 Road accidents are a major problem caused by motor traffic. Find out how many serious accidents resulting in death or injury occurred last year in your local area.

Solving traffic problems

The government and local councils have become very worried about the effects of road transport and traffic jams in towns and cities. They are concerned about:

- human health
- the damage to the environment caused by the noise, air pollution, congestion and traffic jams
- the effects of global warming
- the wastage of time, and of **non-renewable fuels** such as petrol and oil, while engines 'idle' in traffic jams.

How can we solve traffic problems?

In the past, governments believed that building bigger, straighter roads was a way to solve the problems of traffic jams. But those roads also became jammed as more and more traffic used them.

One way to solve the problems is to get people to use forms of transport other than cars. Walking and cycling are better for short journeys. They provide healthy exercise and cause no pollution at all. A bus or train can carry many people at once and causes a lot less pollution than several cars.

How can we discourage car use?

Various ways are being tried to encourage people to stop using their cars, or to use them less. These include:

- increasing the **tax** on petrol and diesel oil to make it more expensive to use a car
- making parking in towns and cities more difficult and more expensive, except for those people who actually live in that town or city
- restricting access to some towns and cities at busy times of the day

What is being done in this picture to help solve traffic problems?

Motor vehicles are not allowed in this street.

- closing some shopping streets to traffic so that people can walk about, safe from traffic – this is called **pedestrianization** of streets
- park-and-ride schemes – large car parks on the outskirts of towns and cities from which shoppers and workers travel into the centre by bus
- traffic-calming schemes, such as **ramps** and **chicanes**, force motor vehicles to travel more slowly through streets where people live, shop or go to school
- trying to encourage more companies to send their goods by rail.

'Metro' systems

In Britain, London is the only city that has a very large network of underground trains. A large network is expensive and difficult to build. But some cities, such as Manchester, Newcastle, Sheffield and Glasgow, have built special, electrically driven light railways, called 'metro' systems. They carry passengers from one part of the city to another quickly, safely and with a minimum of noise and pollution.

The metro system in Croydon, South London

Activities

1 You are a shopkeeper in a street from which motor vehicles have been banned. Give one reason why you might be pleased with this type of traffic planning and one reason why you might not.

2 In the 'rush hour' in many towns and cities, each car often contains only one person. Work with a friend and discuss what could be done to change this. Write down what conclusions you come to.

3 a Collect pictures, or make drawings, of all the methods people use to try to control traffic, such as traffic lights, pedestrian crossings and speed limits.
  b Stick your pictures on a chart or in a book.
  c Write a sentence or two about each one, saying whether or not you think it works, and why.

Do we want a bypass?

A **bypass** road is sometimes built to take all the **through traffic** away from a town or village. Such a road makes people's journeys quicker and safer, while life in the town or village is quieter, safer and less polluted.

Once a bypass is built, new factories and offices often grow up near it, bringing new jobs to the area. But not everyone welcomes a new bypass.

What problems do new roads cause?

Because better roads make journeys easier, new roads can attract more cars and lorries, causing even more noise and pollution. Many motorways have had to be widened in places to take extra traffic.

New roads also take up large areas of land. It may be necessary to knock down houses that are in the way of the route of the new road. Other houses may have the new road close to them, causing noise and pollution for the people who live there.

When the M25 motorway was built all the way around the outskirts of London, road engineers predicted it would carry 80 000 vehicles a day. Within a few months it was carrying 160 000 vehicles a day!

New bypasses take up valuable farmland and may destroy attractive countryside and wildlife. To allow this bypass to be built, the course of a river has been altered.

Unwelcome bypasses

Some people in the bypassed town or village may not welcome the new road. Shopkeepers and the owners of garages, cafés, pubs and other businesses may lose trade because of the reduction in through-traffic.

So, although a bypass may reduce the traffic in a town or village, such a road is extremely expensive and not everyone wants it to be built. What do you think?

Not everyone believes we should keep on building bigger and better roads!

Activities

1 Look at an Ordnance Survey map or road map of your area. Make a list of all the villages, towns and cities which have been bypassed.

2 Imagine there is a proposal to build a bypass around the area where you live. Work with a group of friends and discuss if and where the bypass should be built. Play the parts of the following local people in your discussion:

• a farmer • an elderly person • a traffic planner
• a school headteacher • a lorry driver • a bird-watcher
• the owner of a house on the proposed route

Set up a class discussion.

3 Imagine you are a local planning officer. You receive a proposal to build a large new superstore and cinema next to the local bypass. Make a list of arguments for, and against, allowing the superstore and cinema to be built.

Coasts

What is the **coast**? The coast is the place where the land meets the **oceans** and **seas**. Have you visited any places on the coast? Find them in an atlas.

The seashore

The **seashore** lies along the coast. There are sandy, muddy and rocky seashores, and some seashores are made of **pebbles**. A **beach** is a sloping strip of **sand**, shingle or pebbles at the edge of the sea.

The world has about 320 000 km of coastline, while the coastline of the British Isles stretches for about 14 000 km.

This seashore in southern England has **cliffs** behind it. Cliffs are steep rock faces formed by the action of the **waves**.

This seashore in Grand Canary, Spain, has shifting hills of sand, called **sand dunes**. The sand was blown into dunes by the wind.

Changing coastlines

The shape of the coast changes all the time because of the constant battering by waves and rough seas. In some places, where the rocks are soft, the water often wears away the land, while harder rocks show little sign of wear. In other places, the sea helps to form new land. This new land is made from the tiny pieces of rock the water has carried from other parts of the coast.

Some of the largest **inlets** on the coast are **estuaries**, where rivers flow into the sea. Tiny pieces of mud and sand are swept along by the river and gradually settle on the bottom as the river's **current** is slowed by the incoming waves of the sea. Over many years, the particles form large areas called mudflats. Eventually, these may form new land.

Why are coasts important?

Many people go to the coast for their holidays or to enjoy sports and leisure activities.

Sheltered parts of the coast are used as **ports** for ships and fishing boats.

Some of our food, including fish and shellfish, comes from places on the coast. Salt, oil and natural gas are found in coastal areas.

How have people harmed the coast?

Sadly, human activities are destroying many coastal areas. Thoughtless people leave litter and trample sand dunes, while oil, **sewage** and chemicals from towns, cities and **industries pollute** the beaches and seawater.

An estuary is a river's mouth, where it flows into the sea. This is the estuary of the River Dovey in Wales.

Activities

1 Collect pictures of the different kinds of coastline. Make a class display or scrapbook with your pictures. Write a sentence or two about each picture.

2 Make an illustrated dictionary of words to do with coasts, such as cliff, wave, current, inlet, and so on. Add to your dictionary as you come across new words.

3 Use an atlas or road map to select a part of the coast you would like to visit. Write down the reasons for your choice.

The moving sea

The oceans and seas are never still. The water is constantly moving because of **tides**, waves and currents.

Tides

Twice each day, the level of the ocean or sea rises and water covers the shore. We say that the tide is 'in', or that it is 'high tide'. Twice each day, the level of the seawater falls. The seashore is uncovered and we say the tide has 'gone out', or it is 'low tide'. High tide brings deep water to **harbours** and ports so that large ships can sail in and out, but sometimes a very high tide may cause flooding.

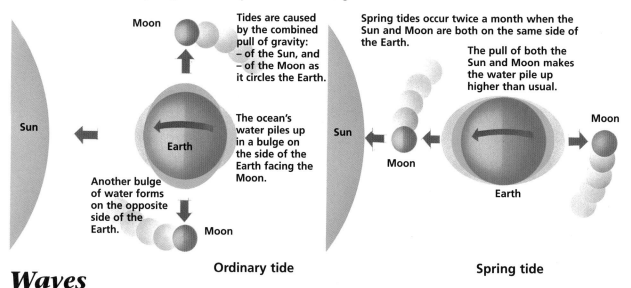

Moon

Tides are caused by the combined pull of gravity:
– of the Sun, and
– of the Moon as it circles the Earth.

Sun

Earth

The ocean's water piles up in a bulge on the side of the Earth facing the Moon.

Another bulge of water forms on the opposite side of the Earth.

Moon

Ordinary tide

Spring tides occur twice a month when the Sun and Moon are both on the same side of the Earth.

The pull of both the Sun and Moon makes the water pile up higher than usual.

Sun

Moon

Moon

Earth

Spring tide

Waves

Waves are big ripples of water caused by the wind. They make the water move up, down and around, but they do not move the seawater from place to place like currents or tides.

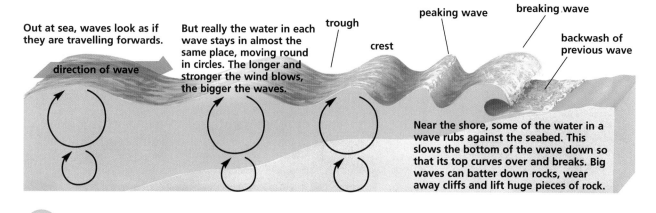

Out at sea, waves look as if they are travelling forwards.

direction of wave

But really the water in each wave stays in almost the same place, moving round in circles. The longer and stronger the wind blows, the bigger the waves.

trough

crest

peaking wave

breaking wave

backwash of previous wave

Near the shore, some of the water in a wave rubs against the seabed. This slows the bottom of the wave down so that its top curves over and breaks. Big waves can batter down rocks, wear away cliffs and lift huge pieces of rock.

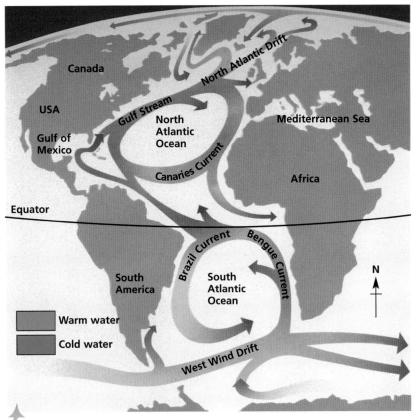

The main currents in the Atlantic Ocean

Currents

Currents are like giant rivers of water moving slowly across the oceans. Most currents are caused by winds that blow in the same direction all the time.

Find the Gulf Stream on the map. It is one of the most important ocean currents. It begins with warm (26–29 °C) water near the **Equator** in the Gulf of Mexico. The warm current then flows up the east coast of the United States, warming the land as it goes. Then it flows across the Atlantic Ocean. What is it called as it flows past the British Isles? The current is warm enough to make the winters in the countries it flows past milder than they would be otherwise.

Activities

1 Work with a friend. Discuss where and when waves, currents and tides can be dangerous to people. What can people do to avoid these dangers when they are at the seaside? Write down what you have decided.

2 • Over most of the Mediterranean Sea, the rise and fall of the tides between high and low water is less than 30 cm.
  • There are no strong currents.
  • Pollution has become a serious problem.

Is there a connection between these three statements? If so, what is it?

3 Western Scotland is usually warmer than eastern England in winter. Why is this? Labrador, in eastern Canada, is about the same distance north of the Equator as Britain. It is also beside the same ocean. Why is Labrador much colder in winter than Britain? Use an atlas. Write down what you have discovered.

Waves at work

Waves carry with them some of the energy and power of the wind. Strong waves hurl pebbles against the cliffs and sea walls. So it is not surprising that waves can wear away, or **erode**, cliffs. They can also damage buildings, sea walls and other structures.

During storms the waves become even more powerful and they can move rocks as big as houses, weighing perhaps 1000 tonnes.

Waves and cliffs

Sea cliffs along a rocky coast often have strange shapes. All these shapes were carved by the waves. As the waves hurl pebbles and lumps of rock at the base of the cliffs, they gradually erode them away. Breaking waves also **compress**, or squeeze, the air trapped in cracks and crevices in the rocks of the cliff. When the waves pull back, the compressed air explodes out, weakening the rock so that eventually lumps break off it. Seawater also weakens and erodes some rocks, such as chalk and limestone, by slowly **dissolving** them.

Cliff erosion

If a cliff is made of soft rocks, such as clay or chalk, it may be eroded quite quickly. Harder rocks, such as granite, are eroded more slowly.

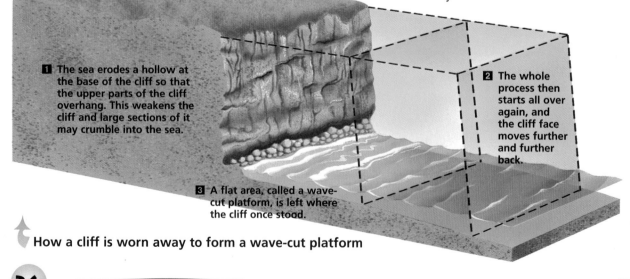

1 The sea erodes a hollow at the base of the cliff so that the upper parts of the cliff overhang. This weakens the cliff and large sections of it may crumble into the sea.

2 The whole process then starts all over again, and the cliff face moves further and further back.

3 A flat area, called a wave-cut platform, is left where the cliff once stood.

How a cliff is worn away to form a wave-cut platform

Bays, headlands and caves

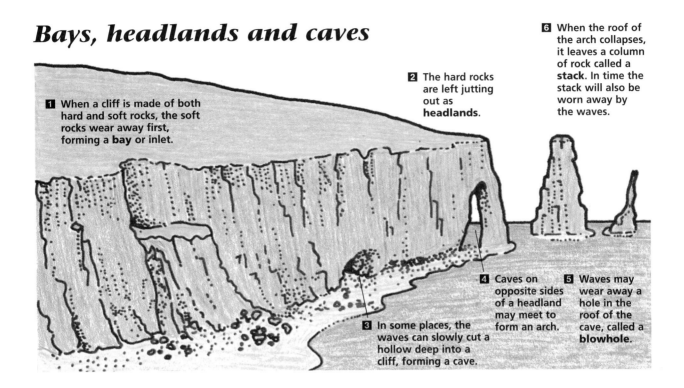

1 When a cliff is made of both hard and soft rocks, the soft rocks wear away first, forming a **bay** or inlet.

2 The hard rocks are left jutting out as **headlands**.

3 In some places, the waves can slowly cut a hollow deep into a cliff, forming a cave.

4 Caves on opposite sides of a headland may meet to form an arch.

5 Waves may wear away a hole in the roof of the cave, called a **blowhole**.

6 When the roof of the arch collapses, it leaves a column of rock called a **stack**. In time the stack will also be worn away by the waves.

Activities

1 Collect pictures showing cliffs, sea caves, stacks and other coastal landforms. Make a class display or scrapbook with your pictures. Write a sentence or two about each one.

2 Use Ordnance Survey maps of coastal areas to identify the coastal features described in this unit.

3 On parts of the coast, cliffs are eroding away. In the past, whole villages have disappeared into the sea. Use reference books and the Internet to find examples of coastal erosion.

Beaches

What is a beach? Beaches are the gently sloping areas of sand, pebbles or mud at the edge of the water, by the sea. Where the coast is sheltered, the beach is often made of sand or mud. At low tide there may be seaweed-covered rocks and rock pools. On open, wind-swept coasts, the beach is usually made of pebbles. Most of the sand has been washed away.

How is sand made?

When the waves erode cliffs, large pieces of rock break off and crash down to the beach below. These large pieces of rock are called **boulders**, and they are rolled backwards and forwards by the waves along with smaller pebbles. Pieces break off the boulders until eventually they are worn down to pebbles. The pebbles are swept backwards and forwards by the waves, tides and currents, which wear them away even more until they are ground into grains of sand.

Other beach materials

Rivers bring millions of tonnes of sand and mud to the oceans and seas every year. This material has been eroded from mountains,

The boulders which have fallen from this cliff will eventually be turned into sand.

hills and rocks inland. This sand and mud may be swept along the coast by tides and currents and may eventually be **deposited** on a beach.

In the **tropics**, many beaches are made almost entirely of tiny fragments of seashells or **coral** washed up from nearby reefs.

These seashells will eventually be worn away to become part of the sand on the beach.

Bricks, pieces of concrete and glass on a beach are slowly worn smooth by the action of the waves, so that they eventually form tiny grains of sand.

Sorting beach materials

On many beaches at low tide, you will find that there are large pieces of rock and pebbles at the top of the beach, and smaller pebbles or sand nearer the water. How was this material sorted?

When a wave breaks on the shore, the water rushes up the beach, taking pebbles and sand with it. The water drains back down the beach in what is called the **backwash**. But the backwash is weak and cannot carry the larger pebbles far, so these are left further up the beach. Smaller pebbles are deposited next, then sand, and finally tiny particles called **silt**. At low tide, you can sometimes see where a sandy beach changes to coarse silt or even fine mud.

At the back of some open, wind-swept beaches are very large, rounded boulders. These were thrown there during violent storms. That is why these beaches are called storm beaches. This storm beach is in western Ireland.

Activities

1 How do boulders break down into pebbles and then sand?
Place a few small pieces of chalk in a plastic jar half full of water. Screw the lid on the jar and shake it vigorously.
a What happens to the pieces of chalk?
b What is left in the bottom of the jar?

2 As we have seen, sand is made of tiny pieces of rock. How many uses of sand can you think of?

3 Use holiday brochures, the Internet and holiday guides to find out where the best sandy beaches are in the world. Make a table of them, arranged by continent or country.

Coastal settlements

Look at an atlas and find how many of the world's largest cities are on the **coast**. There are also large **ports**, industrial towns, fishing villages and holiday **resorts** on the coast. By building and developing these **settlements**, people have changed the **environment** of parts of the coast.

San Francisco in the United States grew into a port because gold was found nearby.

Why do settlements develop on the coast?

Parts of the coast are sheltered from the open **sea** and have natural deep-water **harbours**. These are the best places to launch a boat so villages and ports have grown up in places like this. Portsmouth in southern England, Sydney in Australia and Vancouver in Canada have sheltered, natural harbours.

Tromso city in Norway started life as a port based on fishing and the capture of whales.

Villages also grew near the mouths of rivers, where they could be crossed by a bridge or ford. In many of these places, where land and the sea routes joined, large ports, such as London, Bristol and New York, have developed.

Other coastal towns and cities grew because there were important **resources** or **industries** nearby. Aberdeen in Scotland developed into a major port because of the huge **shoals** of herring in the North Sea. Today, much of its work is connected with the North Sea oil industry. Cardiff in South Wales grew into an industrial city and major port because plentiful supplies of coal were found nearby.

How do ports affect the environment?

Some of the biggest ports in the world developed in the shelter of river **estuaries**. Estuaries are home to many kinds of plants and wildlife. Because estuaries are sheltered from the force of the **waves** and **tides**, they are excellent sites for ports. Dublin in Ireland and Buenos Aires in Argentina developed in the shelter of estuaries. With the development of a port comes the growth of oil refineries, and industries that use the port to bring in their **raw materials** or to **export** their products. But as a port develops, the habitats of plants and animals are destroyed by building work and **pollution**.

Holiday resorts

Villages on coasts with wide sandy **beaches** have grown into holiday resorts. Some of Britain's best-known resorts are Ayr, Blackpool, Bournemouth, Brighton, Llandudno and Tenby. Which coastal holiday resorts do you know?

Why do you think this holiday resort grew? Do holiday resorts damage the environment?

Activities

1 Use your atlas to find the major estuaries of the British Isles. Name the large towns and cities by these estuaries. Which rivers flow into the estuaries? Can you find any large bridges or tunnels crossing these estuaries?

2 Using a road atlas or a map, make lists of coastal villages, towns and cities which have 'mouth', 'bay', 'quay' or 'port' in their name. Make a graph of your results. Which of these is used most often in the names of settlements?

3 With a friend, discuss how holiday resorts damage the environment. Use reference books or the Internet to find out about holiday resorts that are trying to protect the environment.

4 Design your ideal coastal holiday resort. What attractions would it have and where would they be? How will you protect the environment?

Blackpool

Where is Blackpool? Blackpool is the largest and most popular seaside resort in Europe. About 16 million people visit the town each year. Yet, like many other seaside resorts, Blackpool began as a small fishing village.

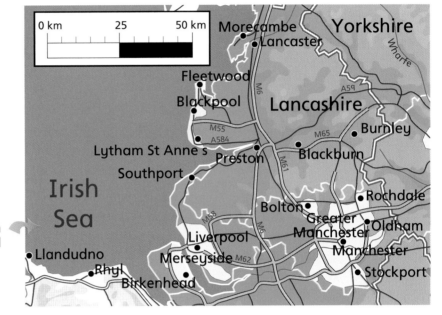

Map of Lancashire and North West England

Early days

By the 1780s, rich families from Manchester were going to Blackpool for what they called the 'bathing season'. It was not long before day-trippers arrived. Most of these travelled by horse and cart, but some people walked more than 60 km on Sundays for a breath of fresh sea air.

In 1846, the railway came to Blackpool, and more and more day-trippers and holidaymakers arrived from the industrial towns of the North. The first of Blackpool's three piers, the North Pier, was opened in 1863. In 1879 it became the first town in Britain to have electric street lighting. The most famous landmark, the Blackpool Tower, was built in 1894. It is 155 m high.

Peak of popularity

Blackpool reached the peak of its popularity as a holiday resort in the 1960s. After that, it began to face increasing competition from cheap **package holidays** to the Mediterranean area and further afield.

These seaside resorts had the big advantage that, unlike Blackpool, they could offer more-or-less guaranteed warmth and sunshine. Today, fewer people visit Blackpool for their annual holidays, but many visit the town for the day or a weekend.

What do visitors do in Blackpool?

As well as the Tower with its ballroom, the attractions include a circus, parks, an art gallery, ice and roller skating rinks, a Sea Life centre, waxworks, a boating lake, model village, golf course and a large amusement park. Each of the piers has its own theatre, and on the beach there are donkey rides and Punch and Judy shows. A tram service runs the full length of Blackpool's 11 km-long promenade, carrying visitors to the various attractions. Blackpool has large numbers of hotels and guesthouses for visitors, as well as discos, bars and restaurants.

Out-of-season activities

During the autumn, from September to late October, 8 km of Blackpool's seafront is a mass of brilliantly lit decorations at night. Millions of people come to admire these world-famous **illuminations**.

Blackpool's famous beach, pier and tower in spring

The Big One, one of the many attractions for visitors to Blackpool

As with all British seaside resorts, the number of visitors to Blackpool in the winter decreases, and **unemployment** increases. Blackpool's hotel-owners and the local council have tried to make the town an all-year resort by holding **conferences**, dance festivals, dog shows and other events, and by putting many of the attractions under cover.

Activities

1 a Find Blackpool on a map or in an atlas. How far away is it from your home? In which direction does it lie from your home?

  b What is the nearest seaside resort to your home? How far away is it and in which direction?

2 Find out about Blackpool using maps, holiday and travel information and the Internet. Design a poster for Blackpool showing its attractions.

3 Interview your grandparents, or other older people, about visiting the seaside when they were children. How did they get there? How long did they stay? What did they do?

4 What is a package holiday? What advantages and disadvantages do package holidays have?

Tenby

Where is Tenby? Tenby is a small seaside resort set on a rocky **headland** in Wales. The town grew up around a castle that was built in the 12th century, protected by massive town walls.

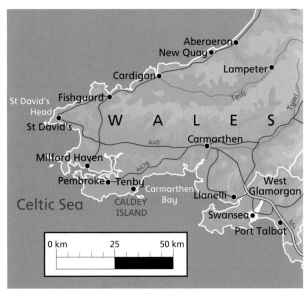

Tenby was a flourishing port in the 14th to 16th centuries. Now it is a bustling holiday resort with a harbour full of sailing boats.

Tenby today

Today, only a few ruins of the castle are left, but the town walls are the most complete in South Wales. Most of the town clusters inside these walls, with the oldest buildings almost touching across the narrow streets. The fishing boats in the harbour no longer set sail to net fish, now they carry **tourists** on sightseeing or fishing trips, or visits to Caldey Island, 5 km offshore. The 18th-century houses overlooking Tenby's harbour have been turned into hotels, while the shops that used to sell equipment for fishermen now sell tourist **souvenirs**.

Holiday attractions

Tourists come to Tenby not only for the traditional bucket-and-spade holiday, but also to enjoy the beautiful scenery of Tenby and its surroundings. The whole area is part of the Pembrokeshire Coast National Park. Walking, diving, boating, jet-skiing, bird-watching and many other leisure activities are enjoyed by visitors.

Traffic problems

Tourism has its drawbacks. As most tourists visit Tenby in the summer, it is difficult to make a living in the winter. Local people are trying to encourage tourists to visit Tenby at all times of the year. In the summer, about 100 000 people pass through Tenby each day. Most of them travel by car, making Tenby's narrow streets dangerous and unpleasant.

Tenby and the surrounding area are so popular that some farmers no longer grow crops such early potatoes. Instead they use their land much more profitably for caravan parks and campsites.

Oil disaster

Tourists who visit a seaside town need to know that the beaches are clean and the sea is safe to bathe in. Tenby has four sandy beaches. In 1996, disaster struck the Pembrokeshire coast. A huge oil tanker, trying to enter the harbour of Milford Haven 24 km away, was shipwrecked. About 72 000 tonnes of crude oil seeped into the sea. Most of the oil was cleaned from the beaches within weeks, but it took several years for the sea and sea-life to recover. Today, the beaches and sea at Tenby are some of the cleanest in Britain.

Activities

1 Find Tenby on a map or in an atlas.
   a How far is it from your home to Tenby?
   b In which direction does it lie?
   c How would you get to Tenby from your home or school?

2 a Carry out a class survey to find out which seaside resorts in Britain the children in your class have visited.
   b Make a chart or block graph of your results.
   c Which resorts have been visited most often?
   d Are these the resorts that are nearest to your home area?

3 What are some of the buildings found only in seaside resorts? Where are these special seaside buildings likely to be?

4 What is done to help to get rid of oil floating on the sea and washed up on beaches? What can be done to help seabirds and other animals that have oil on their bodies? Use reference books or the Internet to help you find out.

Felixstowe, a container port

Until the 1950s, big ships called ocean liners were important for the long-distance **transport** of people. Nowadays, people make most long journeys by aeroplane. The only ocean liners still sailing are cruise ships, which take people on long, floating holidays. However, large numbers of ferry boats and high-speed catamarans are still used for carrying people and **cargoes** over shorter distances. There are also thousands of cargo ships that sail across the world's **oceans** and seas. Although such ships are slow, they can carry huge quantities of cargo over great distances. This is a much cheaper method of transport than using aircraft, which cannot hold as much cargo.

Changing cargoes

Before the 1960s, shipping cargoes were moved in thousands of boxes, sacks and packages. Enormous numbers of **dock**-workers were needed to load and unload ships. It was hard, tiring and badly paid work. Today, bulky goods, such as oil, coal, corn, fertilizers and iron ore, are moved in huge **bulk carriers** or giant **supertankers**. Huge **containers** are used to transport goods by road or rail to and from ports. The containers are carried to other countries by special ships. Bulk carriers, oil supertankers and container ships all need deep water and special equipment for lifting and moving their cargoes. But they need very few workers to manage huge quantities of cargo.

About 100 shipping companies use Felixstowe docks. Their ships visit 370 other ports in 100 countries of the world. More than 3500 lorries visit the port each day to collect or deliver containers. In addition, 140 000 containers travel to Felixstowe by rail each year.

Felixstowe seaside resort and port

Felixstowe is a family seaside resort which first developed around 1900 when the railway was built. It is also the most important cargo and container port in the British Isles. The port received its first cargo ship, a coal-carrying steamer, in 1886, but it was not until the 1950s that Felixstowe port really began to grow.

Environmental costs

The port handles more than 2 million containers a year. Some of the ships that visit Felixstowe can carry 4000 containers.

Felixstowe is Britain's second busiest roll-on/roll-off **freight** terminal. Ferries bring in about 400 000 cargo-carrying lorry trailers a year, while bulk carriers handle oil and other liquids, chemicals and grain.

These giant cranes load and unload the container ships at Felixstowe.

Roll-on/roll-off ferries are ships with large doors at the bow (front) and stern (back), allowing cars and lorries to be driven straight on or off the ship.

Felixstowe is situated at the entrance to the combined estuaries of two rivers – which are they? But as the port has grown, the environment has suffered. There is very heavy road and rail traffic to the port. The estuaries are also important wildlife sites and some of these have been destroyed or reduced in size.

Activities

1 Look at a map showing Felixstowe.
   a Why is it in a good position for a port?
   b What two other ports share the same estuaries as Felixstowe?
   c How far away is Felixstowe from your home, and in which direction?

2 Look at a map or atlas.
   a What country in mainland Europe is the nearest to Felixstowe?
   b How far away is it and in which direction would you have to sail from Felixstowe to reach it?

3 Find out about the holiday resort of Felixstowe. What is the coast like in this part of England?

Dover

Dover is situated at England's closest point to mainland Europe. How far is it from Dover to France? Dover has been England's main port for ships crossing the English Channel for about 2000 years, since the time of the Romans. The Romans built a lighthouse to guide shipping. Its ruined tower still stands on the **cliffs** above the town. Although the town is on a small **bay**, its harbour is artificial.

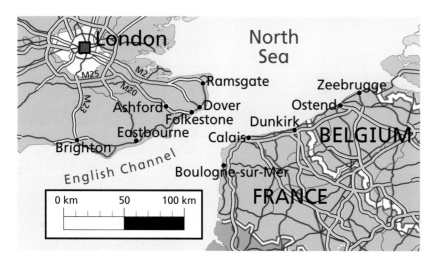

▲ Roll-on/roll-off ferries, high-speed catamarans, bulk cargo ships and cruise ships operate from Dover. Each type of ship has its own special buildings and equipment in the harbour.

More than 16 million passengers, 2.5 million cars, 148 000 coaches and more than 16 million lorries passed through Dover in 2000.

Military port

In the Middle Ages, Dover became one of Britain's main military ports. In the 12th century, a large and powerful castle was built to guard it. The tunnels under the castle, dug during the wars against Napoleon in the 19th century, were used as air-raid shelters during the Second World War. Dover was heavily bombed and shelled from across the Channel.

Busiest passenger port

Today, because it is the port nearest to France and the rest of mainland Europe, Dover is Britain's busiest passenger port, and it is also the busiest ferry port in Northern Europe. From Dover, ferries and catamarans sail to Calais and Dunkirk in France, and to Ostend and Zeebrugge in Belgium. The journey time to Calais, the most popular route, is between 45 and 90 minutes, depending on which type of ship you use.

Communications

Part of Dover's success as a port is its excellent communications with London and the rest of Britain. London is just 125 km away by two **motorways**, the M2 and M20. There are also frequent rail and coach services between London and Dover. Passengers and **vehicles** crossing the Channel from Dover can quickly and easily make their way to all parts of Europe. How far away from Dover are Paris, Brussels, Amsterdam and Frankfurt?

However, the traffic travelling into and out of the port needs large areas of land for roads, railways and car parks. Noise and exhaust fumes are polluting the environment, and **vibrations** caused by heavy lorries are damaging buildings.

In places, the chalk cliffs at Dover are gradually being **eroded** by water, pollution and traffic vibrations. How could the cliffs be protected?

Activities

1 Use a road atlas to help you to work out a route from where you live to Dover.
   a Roughly how far is it?
   b Which roads and motorways would you travel on?
   c Which towns and cities would you travel through or past?

2 List four reasons why Dover is in a good position for a port.

3 Work with a friend. Discuss how the coast is being damaged at and around Dover. Find out what is being done to protect the environment.

Rotterdam, the gateway to Europe

Rotterdam is the largest city in the Netherlands and the world's largest port. How far is it from the sea?

The port of Rotterdam began to develop more than 600 years ago when a small group of fishermen built their huts at a marshy place where the River Maas was joined by a small stream called the Rotte. In 1340, the fishermen dug a canal to send the fish they had caught to other villages. In return, the inland villages sent wheat, cheese and other farm produce for sale in the fishing villages. These cargoes were carried by boat. Trade grew and so did the fishing village, and eventually it became the city of Rotterdam.

The New Waterway

Rotterdam's trade increased when, in 1872, a deep-water **channel**, known as The New Waterway, was dug between Rotterdam and the North Sea. It bypassed the narrow, winding course of the river and allowed ocean-going ships to reach Rotterdam. Cargoes could then be unloaded at Rotterdam and transferred to **barges** which could take them up the River Rhine to Germany, France and Switzerland. At the same time, goods from those countries could be carried down the Rhine to Rotterdam. From there they are exported all over the world.

Rotterdam is also a focus for a **network** of roads and motorways, railway lines and oil pipelines that fan out all over the Netherlands and neighbouring countries.

The port area of Rotterdam

The port

The port has expanded all the way to the sea. Docks, warehouses, stockyards of coal and metal ores, flour mills, factories, shipyards and oil refineries line the waterway.

Europoort

The part of the port nearest the sea is now called Europoort (poort in Dutch means 'gateway'). It was created in 1958 and was seen as 'the Gateway to Europe'. It has expanded greatly, and it can now handle the world's largest bulk carriers of oil, coal, metal ores, chemicals and grain, as well as large container ships and roll-on/roll-off ships and ferries.

Today, Rotterdam handles about 32 000 sea-going ships and 130 000 barges a year.

Loading a container ship and barges at Europoort

Activities

1 Use an atlas and reference books or the Internet to find out:
   a the names of two countries that border the Netherlands.
   b the names of three large cities in the Netherlands.
   c the names of two rivers that reach the sea in the Netherlands.
   d the name of the sea they flow into.
   e what the flag of the Netherlands is like, then draw it.
   f the language spoken in the Netherlands.
   g the population of the Netherlands.

2 Make a collection of items connected with the Netherlands. Here are some suggestions: coins, postage stamps, photographs, labels from cheese packets, garden plant labels or packaging, bus, train or tram tickets.

3 Use an atlas to find out which four ports in the British Isles are nearest to Rotterdam. Which is the nearest British port? How far is it from Rotterdam?

Our friend, the wind

The air around the Earth is always moving. Wind is air moving from one place to another. We use the wind's energy in several ways, but very strong winds can cause serious damage, and sometimes people and animals are killed.

How are winds formed?

The warmer parts of the Earth's surface warm the air above them. Air that is warmed is lighter than the surrounding air, so it rises. In other places, the air cools and becomes heavier so that it sinks. The wind blows because cold air moves to replace the warmer air that has risen.

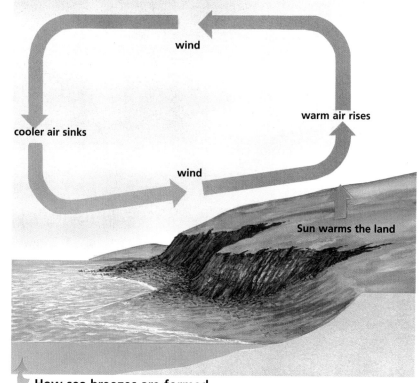

wind

cooler air sinks

warm air rises

wind

Sun warms the land

How sea breezes are formed

From earliest times, sailing boats and ships were pushed along by the wind, as yachts and dinghies are today.

Sea breezes

Winds often start blowing near the sea. Sometimes on a hot day you can feel this when a cool breeze blows from the sea towards the **beach**. On a hot day, the land warms up more quickly than the sea. Air above the warm land rises, so cooler air from over the sea moves in to take its place. At night, the wind blows in the opposite direction because the land cools more quickly than the sea.

The power of the wind

People have used the power of the wind for thousands of years. Long ago, the Chinese flew kites on a windy day to frighten their enemies.

The earliest windmills were used to pump water or to grind corn into flour. There are still a few of these old windmills working today, but many modern windmills are used as wind **turbines** or wind **generators**. They have large blades, like propellers, and when these turn they drive generators that produce electricity. Unlike coal, oil and natural gas, the wind is a source of energy which does not **pollute** the air and which will never run out. The wind is one kind of **renewable energy**.

Wind pumps are used in many parts of the world for pumping water from wells and drainage ditches.

Activities

1 Collect, or draw, pictures showing the good and bad effects of the wind. Write a description of what each picture shows.

2 a Make a list of all the words you can think of which describe the wind.
  b Make a list of words that describe temperature.
  c Make a list of words that describe rainfall.
  d Which is the longest list?

3 People sometimes make or plant wind-breaks. What is a wind-break and where and when would a wind-break be useful?

4 Much of the world was explored with the help of the wind. Use reference books or the Internet to find out more about explorers who used sailing ships, and about their journeys.

Wind strength

We describe the wind by talking about its strength or speed, and the direction in which it is blowing.

Wind direction

How can we tell which way the wind is blowing? We can see the direction in which the wind is blowing by looking at a weather vane on a tower or church. A wind is named by the compass direction from which it blows. So a north wind is one that blows from the north towards the south. Where does a south wind blow from?

At airports, airfields and ports there may be a windsock. This is a long cloth tube through which the wind is funnelled. It shows both the direction and strength of the wind. The straighter the sock, the stronger the wind.

What are prevailing winds?

The most frequent, or **prevailing**, winds in Britain are westerly. These move across the Atlantic Ocean bringing windy, wet **weather**. Because of this, the wettest parts of Britain are the high mountains and moorlands in the west. Land east of these areas is drier.

The Beaufort scale

We can estimate the speed of the wind by seeing what effect it has on smoke, flags and tree branches. Weather forecasters often use a scale worked out by Admiral Sir Francis Beaufort in 1805 for measuring wind speed at sea. His scale has been altered for use on land. The **Beaufort scale** goes from 0, which is dead calm with no wind at all, to 12 and over, which is a **hurricane**.

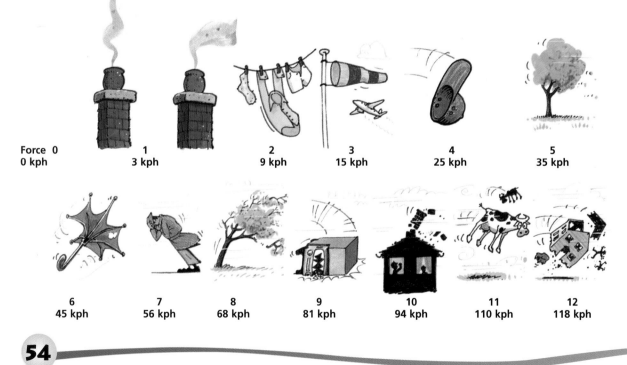

Force 0	1	2	3	4	5
0 kph	3 kph	9 kph	15 kph	25 kph	35 kph

6	7	8	9	10	11	12
45 kph	56 kph	68 kph	81 kph	94 kph	110 kph	118 kph

How can we measure wind speed?

It is important to describe wind speeds accurately, especially for the safety of boats and ships, aircraft and oil rigs. The scientific instrument for measuring wind speed is called an 'anemometer'. On an anemometer, four little cups turn in the wind. They are attached, by a shaft, to a meter rather like a car speedometer, or to a scale. The harder the wind blows, the faster the cups of the anemometer turn, and the higher the reading on the meter.

An anemometer

Can you see the anemometer in this weather station?

Activities

1 Prevailing winds over Britain come mainly from the west, especially in winter. Look at an atlas. Why do you think the prevailing winds often bring wet weather?

2 Study the weather forecasts on the television or in a newspaper. How are the wind strength and direction shown on these forecasts? Draw some of the symbols used.

3 How do buildings affect wind strength and direction? Plan an investigation to find out what happens to the wind on a windy day around the buildings of your school.

4 Using a stick, some tissue paper and sticky tape, design and make a device that will show you the wind strength and direction. Draw your device and explain how it works.

Hurricanes

What is a hurricane? There are strong winds all over the world, but the most powerful winds are hurricanes and **tornadoes**. They are most common in hot places, such as the **tropics**.

A hurricane is called a 'tropical cyclone' around the Indian Ocean and Oceania, and a **typhoon** in the Pacific Ocean.

How do hurricanes form?

Hurricanes usually begin over **tropical** parts of the world's **oceans** where the temperature is more than 27 °C. Scientists believe that hurricanes form when the air is much warmer than the surface of the ocean. The winds then pick up huge amounts of energy and **water vapour** as they rush towards the land. When the wind speed reaches 120 kph the storm is called a hurricane.

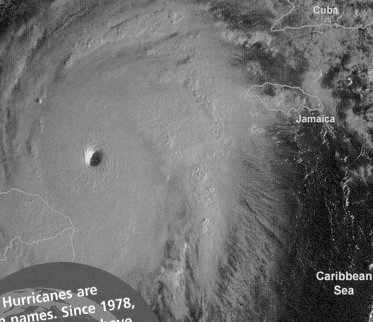

Cuba

Jamaica

Caribbean Sea

A hurricane is a whirling mass of air that can be as much as 900 km across and 10 km high. Inside it, the mass of wind and clouds spirals upwards. At the centre or 'eye' of the hurricane (the clear patch in the centre), the skies are clear, the temperatures are high and the air is fairly calm. The strongest winds, with speeds of up to 350 kph, occur immediately around the eye of the hurricane.

Hurricanes are given names. Since 1978, weather scientists have drawn up a list of alternate boys' and girls' names in alphabetical order. Each time a new hurricane is discovered, it is given the next name on the list. Has your name been used yet?

Wind and rain

It takes several days for the hurricane to travel from the ocean, where it was formed, to the land. On average, a hurricane lasts for a week or two. Hurricanes produce massive amounts of rain (300–600 mm).

Hurricane damage

As it crosses the ocean, the hurricane pushes up huge **waves**. The water level near or under a hurricane can be 5 m higher than the water level in the ocean around. When these waves reach land, they can cause serious flood damage. Boats are lifted out of **harbours**, flung over sea walls and smashed to pieces far inland. Trees are uprooted by the hurricane winds, houses are destroyed, lorries are lifted off the road and telephone poles are snapped off. Anyone who is caught outside has little chance of survival.

Hurricane damage occurs mainly on the **coast** and on islands. A hurricane usually weakens and dies out fairly quickly once it is away from the ocean. This is because it gets all its energy and moisture from the sea.

Hurricane Mitch destroyed buildings and bridges and killed thousands of people in Central America. In Honduras, 1.7 million people were affected by flooding and landslides caused by the hurricane.

Activities

1 Collect newspaper cuttings describing the damaging effects of the wind in various parts of the world. If you can, use the Internet to find out more details of these events.

2 Imagine you are living in an area that has been hit by a hurricane. Write an account of what happened to you, your family and your home. Describe what you were thinking when the hurricane was at its worst. Describe the scene that met you when you went out after the hurricane had passed by.

3 Collect pictures, newspaper cuttings and printouts of information from the Internet describing the destruction caused by a hurricane. If you can, plot the route of the hurricane on a map.

Tornadoes

In the United States tornadoes are often called 'twisters'.

What is a tornado? Tornadoes are small, extremely powerful **whirlwinds**. They form suddenly into a rapidly twisting funnel of air and cloud that stretches from the bottom of a thundercloud to the ground.

How do tornadoes form?

Like a hurricane, a tornado is powered by rising **humid air**. But a tornado is narrower, faster and more violent than a hurricane and it destroys everything in its path. Tornadoes often occur in small groups and, unlike hurricanes, are often found far inland. Although a tornado travels across the land at speeds of only 30 to 65 kph, the wind speeds inside the tornado can reach 800 kph. A tornado may measure anything from just a few metres to more than 100 m across. It can travel for more than 200 km before it uses up all its energy.

Although a tornado affects only a small area, it can be more destructive than any other kind of weather. It is a killer!

A large tornado destroys everything in its path. It sucks up dust, sand, cars, buildings, and even people and animals, like a gigantic vacuum cleaner. Occasionally, a tornado lasts for several hours, but most last for only a few minutes.

Where do tornadoes occur?

Although tornadoes can develop in most parts of the world, they are most common in the United States. On average, about 1000 tornadoes occur there every year. Tornadoes also happen regularly in parts of Canada, Argentina, China, Australia, south-west Asia and even Europe. In Britain, there are between 15 and 30 small tornadoes each year.

Waterspouts

If a tornado forms over a **lake** or the sea it is called a **waterspout**. The funnel of a waterspout looks white because it contains tiny droplets of water that have cooled and **condensed** from the whirling funnel of air.

Waterspouts usually last only a few minutes. Although they are less powerful than land tornadoes, some waterspouts have wrecked boats, jetties and houses along the coast.

This waterspout formed over the sea near the island of Bermuda. Which ocean surrounds Bermuda?

Activities

1 Make a table to compare hurricanes and tornadoes. Include how and where they form, their size, their destructiveness and any other similarities and differences you can find.

2 Look on the Internet to find out more about waterspouts. Draw a diagram to show how a waterspout is formed.

3 Collect pictures and newspaper cuttings showing the path of destruction caused by a tornado. If you can, plot the route of the tornado on a map.

The British Isles

ATLANTIC OCEAN

SHETLAND ISLANDS

ORKNEY ISLANDS

NORTH SEA

OUTER HEBRIDES

Isle of Skye

Isle of Mull

● Inverness

● Aberdeen

SCOTLAND

● Edinburgh

● Glasgow

R. Foyle

● Londonderry

NORTHERN IRELAND

● Belfast

Isle of Man

● Newcastle

R. Ouse

R. Shannon

REPUBLIC OF IRELAND

R. Barrow

■ Dublin

IRISH SEA

● Blackpool

Liverpool ●

● Leeds

● Manchester

● Limerick

● Kilkenny

R. Trent

● Nottingham

● Cork

WALES

R. Severn

● Birmingham

R. Great Ouse

● Cambridge

● Felixstowe

ENGLAND

Tenby ●

Swansea ●

Cardiff ●

● Bristol

● Oxford

R. Thames

■ London

CELTIC SEA

● Reading

● Dover

ATLANTIC OCEAN

● Exeter

Portsmouth ●

● Brighton

● Calais

Isle of Wight

ENGLISH CHANNEL

0 km 50 100 km

Guernsey

FRANCE

Jersey

60

The world

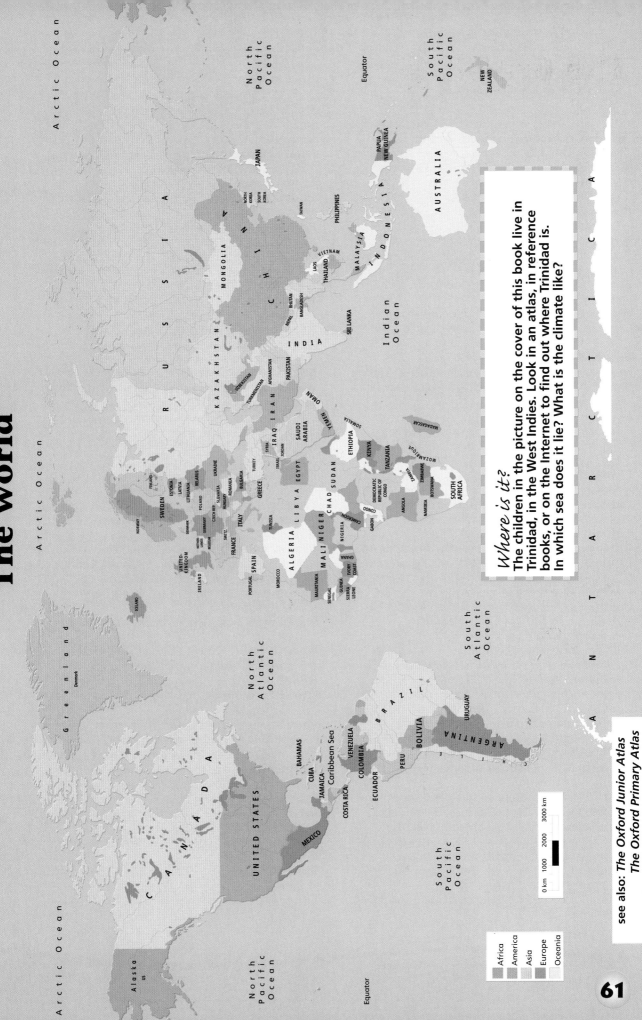

Where is it?

The children in the picture on the cover of this book live in Trinidad, in the West Indies. Look in an atlas, in reference books, or on the Internet to find out where Trinidad is. In which sea does it lie? What is the climate like?

see also: *The Oxford Junior Atlas*
The Oxford Primary Atlas

Africa
America
Asia
Europe
Oceania

0 km 1000 2000 3000 km

Glossary

Acid rain Rain that contains harmful acids because it has dissolved waste gases from the air.

Adapt To become suited to the environment.

Backwash The water which flows back down the beach after a wave has broken on the shore.

Barge A type of boat that carries goods on a river or canal.

Bay A place where the shore curves inwards.

Beach The loose sand, shingle or other materials at the edge of a sea or lake.

Beaufort scale A scale used to measure the strength of the wind.

Blowhole A hole in the roof of a sea cave through which a blast of air is pushed when a wave breaks inside the cave.

Boulder A large piece of rock.

Bulk carrier A ship or vehicle designed to carry a large number of identical goods or a large volume of liquid or grain.

Bypass A road built around a town or city to reduce the traffic in the town or city centre.

Cargo Goods carried by a ship, aeroplane or other type of vehicle.

Channel A groove or passage along which water flows.

Chicane A route where obstacles have been placed to make traffic travel slowly.

Chlorine A gas used to clean water.

Cliff A steep rock face, especially on the coast.

Climate The average weather of a region of the Earth throughout the year.

Coast Where the land meets the sea.

Compress To squeeze something to make it smaller.

Condense When a gas turns into a liquid when it is cooled, we say it condenses.

Conference A meeting of people for a discussion.

Container A large metal box that is used for transporting goods by road, rail or sea.

Continent One of the seven large areas of land on the Earth's surface.

Coral A hard substance made of the skeletons of tiny sea animals.

Current The movement of air or water in a particular direction.

Dam A wall built from concrete, soil or other materials across a river to form a reservoir.

Deposition The way in which a river, the sea or the wind drops material it has been carrying.

Desert A dry region with very few plants.

Dissolve To make a solid substance break up and disappear into a liquid.

Dock A place where ships are loaded, unloaded or repaired.

Drought A long period of dry weather.

Dual carriageway A road with two lanes in either direction, separated by a barrier.

Environment Your surroundings.

Equator The imaginary line around the middle of the Earth.

Erode To wear away land by water, wind or ice.

Erosion The wearing away of land by moving water, wind or ice.

Estuary The wide mouth of a river where fresh water meets sea water.

Evaporate When a liquid turns into a gas as it is heated.

Export To sell goods to another country.

Famine A time when there is not enough food for the people of an area.

Felt A type of thick fabric.

Fertile Moist, rich soil where crops grow well.

Filter beds Layers of sand and gravel that are used to separate insoluble particles from water in a water treatment works.

Flight path The route followed by an areoplane between airports or airfields.

Fluoride A substance added to clean water to help to protect teeth from decay.

Freight Goods transported from place to place.

Generator A machine that produces electricity.

Glacier A slow-moving river of ice.

Global warming A gradual increase in the average temperature of the Earth's climate caused by certain kinds of air pollution.

Groundwater Water in the rocks below the Earth's surface.

Harbour A place where ships and boats can shelter or unload.

Hardwood A type of wood that is strong. Mahogany, teak and rosewood are hardwoods.

Headland Land sticking out into the sea.

Humid air Air that contains a large amount of water vapour.

Hurricane A powerful swirling storm found in tropical parts of the Atlantic Ocean (called tropical cyclones in Asia or typhoons in Oceania).

Illuminations Streets decorated with lights.

Industry The making of things in factories or workshops.

Inlet A small opening in the coastline.

Irrigation Transporting water from rivers, lakes, wells or reservoirs to the land so that crops grow well.

Lake A hollow in the land which is filled with water.

Lane [1] A narrow road. [2] A strip of road marked out to keep streams of traffic separate.

Latrine A very basic type of toilet.

Monsoon A strong wind in and around the Indian Ocean which brings heavy rain in summer.

Motorway A wide road built for fast-moving cars, lorries and coaches.

Network A system consisting of many lines or parts, such as roads or railway tracks.

Nomad A person who lives and works on the move from one place to another.

Non-renewable fuels Fuels that cannot be replaced once all the supplies have been used.

Oasis A place in a desert where water can be found.

Ocean One of five great areas of salt water which cover nearly three-quarters of the Earth's surface.

Package holiday A holiday organized by a travel company.

Pebble A small, rounded stone.

Pedestrian Someone who is walking.

Pedestrianization Closing a street to motor traffic so that it can be used only by people on foot.

Plantation An area of land where a crop, such as tea, coffee, sugar cane or rubber or fruit trees are grown, usually for sale abroad.

Pollute To make dirty.

Pollution When substances such as air, water or the soil are spoiled or made dirty by people.

Port A place where ships stop to load and unload their cargo.

Power station A large building where electricity is produced.

Prevailing wind A wind that almost always blows from the same direction.

Purify To make completely clean.

Rainforest A forest that grows in a place that is hot and rainy all the year round.

Ramp A slope between two levels.

Raw materials Materials which are used to make new material.

Renewable energy Energy sources that are never used up.

Reservoir A lake built by people to store water.

Resort A place where people go for a holiday.

Resource A useful or valuable thing.

Routeway A way of getting from one place to another.

Sand Tiny grains of rock or pieces of shell.

Sand dune A hill formed by wind-blown sand.

Sea A very large area of salt water.

Seashore The land close to the sea, especially the part between high and low water marks.

Settlement A place, such as a village, town or city, where people live.

Sewage The waste material and liquid from buildings, carried away by drains and sewers.

Shingle A lot of small pebbles.

Shoal A large number of fish swimming together.

Silt Small particles, finer than sand but coarser than mud or clay.

Souvenir Something that you keep because it reminds you of a person, place or event.

Spring A place where water flows out of the ground.

Stack A pillar of rock in the sea near cliffs.

Supertanker A very large ship that carries liquid cargo such as oil.

Tax Money that people have to pay to the government.

Through traffic Traffic that passes through a place without stopping.

Tides The rise and fall of the level of the oceans and seas twice a day.

Tornado (or twister) A very violent whirlwind.

Tourist A person who visits a place or country for pleasure.

Transport Ways of taking people or goods from one place to another.

Tropical In or from the tropics.

Tropics The regions near the Equator that have a hot climate all the year round.

Turbine A type of fan which is turned by steam, water pressure or the wind.

Typhoon A weather system that brings very powerful winds and torrential rain, and causes widespread destruction.

Unemployment Being without a job.

Vehicle Something which transports people, animals or things.

Vibration A shaking backwards and forwards.

Waterhole A pool of water from which animals drink regularly.

Water main The pipe that carries water to a building.

Waterspout A tornado over the sea.

Water vapour The gas that forms when water is heated.

Wave A regular movement of the surface of water caused by the wind.

Weather How hot or cold, wet or dry, moving or still the air is at a particular time.

Well A hole that has been dug or drilled into the ground to reach underground water, oil or gas.

Whirlwind A strong wind that blows round and round.

Index